S0-AZV-877

WHEN WINTER COMES

ROBERT MAASS

HENRY HOLT AND COMPANY · NEW YORK

Henry Holt and Company, LLC, *Publishers since 1866*
115 West 18th Street, New York, New York 10011

Henry Holt is a registered
trademark of Henry Holt and Company, LLC

Copyright © 1993 by Robert Maass. All rights reserved.
Distributed in Canada by H. B. Fenn and Company Ltd.

Library of Congress Cataloging-in-Publication Data
Maass, Robert. When winter comes / Robert Maass.
Summary: Simple text and photographs introduce winter
and its various activities.
1. Winter—Juvenile literature. [1. Winter.] I. Title
QB637.8.M3   1993   508—dc20   93-7146

ISBN 0-8050-4926-6
First published in hardcover in 1993 by Henry Holt and Company
First Owlet paperback edition—1996
Printed in Hong Kong

10   9   8   7   6   5   4   3

Winter comes on the shortest day of the year

when the temperature drops

and it's time to bundle up.

Snow blankets
the ground.
The air is cold,
water freezes, and
the world looks
transparent and still.

Sleds, stacked high, speed down hills

and snowballs fly.

Winter's holidays are a time
for giving and receiving.
Chanukah is the festival of lights.

Christmas presents
bring delight.

Winter's bounty brings
hearty root vegetables

to simmer in soup.

Birds search hard
for a winter meal,
so people often
lend a hand,

which helps
other creatures too.

Animals wear their
winter coats and leave
pawprints in the snow.

When winter comes,
deep snow cushions
a football tackle

and kids gather for a hockey game on a frozen country pond.

Woodpiles shrink

as logs are burned for cozy fires.

Hats of all shape,
size, and color keep
heads and bodies warm.

There are winter chores

and winter pleasures,

winter sports to learn

and moms with energy to burn.

Everybody knows no two
snowflakes are alike.
Nor are any two hearts.

The late winter days
of snow and cold,
of snowmen

and warmth within,

bring thoughts of sunnier days and the coming of the spring.